Money-Smart Kid$

Also by Gail Vaz-Oxlade

It's Your Money
Never Too Late
Debt-Free Forever

Money-Smart Kid$

Teach Your Children Financial Confidence and Control

GAIL VAZ-OXLADE

Collins

Money-Smart Kids
Copyright © 2011 by Gail Vaz-Oxlade.
All rights reserved.

Published by Collins, an imprint of HarperCollins Publishers Ltd

First published in Canada by Collins as an e-book original: 2011
This Collins trade paperback edition: 2011

This book is based on *The Money Tree Myth* by Gail Vaz-Oxlade,
first published by Stoddart Publishing in 1996.

HarperCollins books may be purchased for educational, business,
or sales promotional use through our Special Markets Department.

HarperCollins Publishers Ltd
2 Bloor Street East, 20th Floor
Toronto, Ontario, Canada
M4W 1A8

www.harpercollins.ca

Library and Archives Canada Cataloguing in Publication
information is available.

ISBN 978-1-44341-229-2

Printed and bound in the United States
RRD 9 8 7 6 5 4 3 2 1

To my beautiful children, Alexandra and Malcolm,
who have taught me all I know about mommyhood.
It has been a privilege to be your teacher and your guide.
I love you two bits!

Contents

Money-Smart Kid$

Introduction

E veryone thinks kids should learn about money: how it works and how to manage it. But everyone also seems to think it's someone else's job to teach kids about money. Money lessons should be taught at school. Borrowing should be taught by lenders. Banking should be taught by, well, bankers.

The best place for kids to learn about how money works—and the role it should play in their lives—is at home. While financial literacy is a hot topic, there have been times when other hot topics took the front burner. Remember the food pyramid? It's still being taught at school, which is why we no longer have a child-obesity problem. Oh, wait . . . that's not right!

When kids are introduced to the food pyramid at school, they learn all about which foods are healthiest and how much of each kind of food they should include in their diets. But telling kids to eat five to seven servings of fruits and veggies each day has little impact if, when they get home, mommy and daddy serve up a hot dog, a bag of chips, and a tin of pop for dinner. Out the window goes the lesson just learned, and kids come to know that the stuff they're taught at school is irrelevant to their lives.

And so it is with money. We can talk until we're blue in the face about how important it is to save, but if our children don't see us saving at home, they won't learn the lesson. We can talk about becoming smart consumers, but if parents whip out their credit cards every time something takes their fancy—or worse, because a kid demands it—they're teaching kids they don't have to prioritize; they can buy whatever they want, whenever they want it, as long as they have enough credit.

But growing up in a financially sound home doesn't automatically translate into financial success for kids. Children don't learn about money by osmosis. They need to be taught the rules of good money management. They need lots of practice to incorporate those lessons into their lives. They need to be able to fail safely and adjust their thinking as they learn about how money works. And there's a lot to learn. So we should start early.

Want to teach your children to be more financially successful? Want them to avoid living from paycheque to paycheque? Want them to steer clear of crippling student loans and credit card debt? Then it's time to take the reins of your child's financial education firmly in hand. If you're hesitant because you think teaching kids to be smart about money is a big task—one that you might flub—relax. As your child's first and most natural teacher, you are in a unique position to be able to help, and you can do it in very small steps.

Think back to the nurturing you gave when your baby took his first steps. You encouraged him by celebrating even his smallest successes. You helped take away the fear by letting him hold your hands. You laughed, played, and had fun. And in no time at all he was walking. Raising Money-Smart Kids takes much the same approach: the learning should be fun, it should be given consistently, and it should be rewarded. Learning about money should feel good.

If you have more than one child, you know that no two children learn in the same way or at the same speed. You, more than anyone else, understand how your children learn; you adapt to each of your children's unique needs so that over time they grow stronger and more confident. It's not about boring them to death with money lessons. It's about engaging them in conversations, sharing ideas, and reinforcing positive behaviour.

Since children love to be part of everything their parents do, day-to-day life offers you a multitude of opportunities for teaching them about how money works and the role it should play in their lives. But trying to decide what to teach and when can be daunting. With this book, you now have a guide to help you decide.

I'll help you figure out how to best use an allowance: when you should give it, how much you should give, and how to set some expectations. I'll suggest specific money lessons that you can teach at each age and stage of your child's life, from toddler to teenager. I'll show you how to teach kids about credit so they learn to use it smartly and to not make the mistakes some adults make. And I'll help you set the habit of saving in place so it's a no-brainer by the time your kid goes to work full-time. Oh, yeah, shopping . . . we'll talk about that too!

I know you want the best for your kids. Like me,

you want to make sure your children can stand on their own two feet and make good decisions about what to do with their money. If you follow the plan in this book, your children will be smart about money; they'll know what they can, should, and won't do for it and with it.

Here we go.

1. Allowance

If you want your kids to learn about money, you've got to put some in their hands. Children are the most concrete of learners. Without some actual dollars and cents to work with, everything you say will be a discussion "in theory." Give a child an allowance and you move from the theoretical to the practical, from thinking to doing.

Giving kids money is easy . . . you've been doing it for years. Whether you hand over coins for your kid to buy a can of pop or you take her into a store to pick out a new pair of shoes, you are constantly spending money.

"Mommy, can I have an ice-cream cone?"

"Dad, my hockey stick broke."

"Mom, I need money for the book fair at school."

"My pants are too short."

"I need a haircut."

"My calculator is broken."

The idea of an allowance is to put some of the money you routinely spend on your child directly into her hands so that she can learn how to manage it for herself. It's about transferring responsibility for financial decision-making to your child so that she can get some practice. Given regularly, an allowance not only provides kids with the bucks they need to experiment with saving and spending, it also gives them the responsibility for keeping their money safe and using it wisely. Over time, even a modest allowance will get kids thinking about the value of money and how to make their dollars go further.

The alternative to an allowance, and a trap for most parents, is the dole system. That's when your kid asks for some cash and you dole it out. Since the dole system has no limit, there is no reason for a child to set priorities or make a decision on relative value. Another downside to the dole system is that you remove all control from your child. You get to decide which of his requests is valid enough for consideration, and your child feels like a beggar. Your child learns the Gimme Game really well, and you grow resentful of the constant requests for cash.

"But Mom, I only need $2."

"Gee, Dad, it only costs $5."

"Can I have another quarter? Another dollar? Another $100?"

If you're currently on the dole system and don't fully appreciate what it's costing you, keep track of all the money you hand over to your kid in a month. Yup, write it down. Never mind whining about what a pain it is to do this. DO IT and you'll see exactly how much money your kids are getting each month. You might be surprised by how large your kid's allowance is!

Set Expectations

To learn how to manage money responsibly, children need an income they can rely on—one given at regular intervals. The experience of handling a steady flow of cash will teach many fundamental skills, including how to plan ahead, how to set goals (both short and long term), and how to save.

While I'm all for giving children an allowance, I also believe very strongly that you need to set some expectations for what kids will do with their money. This is the step that most parents skip, so they lose the wonderful opportunity an allowance offers to teach new skills and attitudes.

If you just hand your child an allowance without

any guidelines, she'll learn that she can spend money on anything she wants every week. The liberty to spend at will does nothing to teach good money management. In fact, it isn't a liberty afforded to us as adults. Since we are required to spend a certain amount of our hard-earned money on fixed expenses, regardless of what we want to buy ourselves—we have to keep a roof over our heads and our children fed—allowing kids to do as they will with their entire allowance isn't a true representation of money management in the real world.

Initially, the allowance you give to young children will help them learn how to count coins; how to divvy up their money into categories like savings, sharing, and spending; and how to make small purchases. Over time, as their allowance increases, you'll tie more planned spending into their allowance expectations: they'll become responsible for paying for their own books through school programs, for buying their own school supplies, for budgeting for their after-school activities.

In learning how to manage money, children need to see that there are a variety of purposes for money, not just the immediate gratification of spending it. Spending is a part of the equation, but so, too, is saving and sharing with others less fortunate.

Look at an allowance as having three components: (1) the part to be saved, (2) the part to be shared, and (3) the part to be spent. This third part of the allowance equation can itself be broken down into two parts: first, the spending kids want to be able to do on a whim (their "mad money"); and second, the spending they intend to do based on specific expenses and expressly stated goals (their planned spending). Spending on a whim comes naturally to most people. Saving, sharing, and planned spending are all ideas that have to be introduced, practised, and reinforced.

Setting Up Magic Jars for Kids

One way to clearly differentiate between the different purposes for money is to set up money holders for each purpose. Believe it or not, this is where the idea for the Magic Jars came from. I recommend that parents use four clearly labelled jars: Savings, Sharing, Planned Spending, and Mad Money. Get your kids involved in labelling and decorating their jars. It's not just a great craft activity; it also gives them a sense of ownership.

The reason the jars work for children (and apparently for adults too) is that they make the finite nature of money visual. There is only so much. If you spend it on one thing, you won't have it to spend on another. When the money is gone, you have to stop spending. As adults, we've lost touch with the idea that money is finite because we've fallen into the trap of using credit to fill the gap. Living on the Magic Jars puts people back in touch with the fact that money is a finite resource and that you have to plan if you want to get to the end of the month before you get to the end of the money.

How Much?

The amount you choose to give your child will depend on how much you can afford, your child's age, and what you expect your child to do with her allowance. If, for example, the most you can afford is $5 a week, so be it. While many parents are stuck on the $2-a-week allowance, just think about what $2 can buy in this day and age (after you deduct for saving and sharing), and you'll have a good idea of how effective (NOT) that amount will be in teaching money management.

Ask your child to list the five most important things he wants to do with his money. If he is an avid reader and wishes to buy his own books, he'll need more than a child who is only interested in candy.

Naturally, younger children need, and are capable of handling, less money. If all your child is buying is candy and the occasional toy, you may want to start her off with a relatively small sum. At five years old, 50¢ a week may be more than sufficient.

When you first start giving an allowance to young children—those aged six to 10—I suggest that you use your child's age as a guide, giving a dollar a week for each year. So a seven-year-old would get $7 a week. You're the best judge of the amount that will be most appropriate for your child. Just remember that it needs to be enough so that your child can save, share, and spend. And know that over time, as you increase your child's financial responsibilities, you will increase the allowance to cover specific spending categories like school supplies, clothing, and gift-giving.

Make It Easy for Kids

When you give the allowance, and how, will affect your kid's development of good money-management skills. Younger children find it easier to handle money if they are given a small amount every week.

Consider what time of the week is best. If your experience says that giving an allowance at the beginning of the weekend means it's all gone by Monday, then give it on Monday or Wednesday. While you want your child to accept responsibility, young children need some help in developing the skills. The timing of the allowance may make all the difference.

Children who are older and have established many of the habits of budgeting should be asked when and how often they prefer to receive their allowance. While some kids like getting a little money each week, others may prefer a lump sum that allows them to plan spending for the month.

Whatever allowance schedule you establish with your children, make sure you stick to it. It's demeaning for anyone to have to constantly ask for money. And providing the allowance on time will send a subtle message about the value of honouring commitments.

Also think about the denominations in which you'll give the allowance. If you give your 10-year-old all his money as a single bill, he'll have trouble implementing his budgeting plan without hitting a store to make change. Giving him smaller denominations means he will find it easier to set aside the money for the various parts of his budget like saving, sharing, and planned spending.

How Much Goes in Each Jar?

The rule of thumb for saving is that you should save 10% of your income. (This does vary depending on the age at which you start saving, but it's a good guideline, so we'll stick with it.) If your child gets $6 a week, the first expectation to set is that 60¢ needs to be put in the Savings Jar.

The rule of thumb for sharing is whatever you make it; in my house it was that you should put aside 5% of your income for those who are less fortunate, so if this is something that is important in your household, then into the Sharing Jar should go 30¢ (or whatever amount works in your family).

Now comes the hard part. What percentage of the remaining money should be planned spending versus mad money? That depends on whether your child is expected to pay specific costs for herself and what long-term spending goals she has.

Let's say, for example, that you provide your child with a large enough allowance to pay for her bus fare to and from school each week. That money should be set aside in the Planned Spending Jar to be used each day as needed. If you expect your child to buy gifts for special occasions from her allowance, you'll have to figure out how many gifts are bought each year, and how much of her allowance needs to be set aside each week so the money will be there when the special occasions roll around. (You may also have to set up extra jars so your child can set the money aside visually.)

Your child might also have a special purchase in mind, like a new iPod. Help her determine how much she needs to put aside each week so that dream can become a reality. And help her come up with a system for monitoring her progress so she stays motivated. The rest of the money is mad money. She can spend it, or she can put it towards her planned spending goal (the iPod). She can do anything she wants with it!

When my daughter, Alex, was heading off on a European trip with her school chums, I paid for the trip and she had to come up with the spending money. As the date of departure grew closer, we were talking about how much she had, and she was commenting on how her friends were scrambling to find money. "But they've been shopping," she said. "Every time I wanted to buy something, I thought about the trip, and then I thought about what I wanted more—that thing in the store or the money for the trip." See, it works. Teach your kids that money is a finite resource and they will weigh their infinite spending opportunities to figure out what they really want!

Tying Allowances to Chores and School Work

If there were strings attached to the money you received as a child, those memories will have a strong bearing on the strings you attach to your children's money. Perhaps you were never given an allowance and had to work for every penny you got. Your allowance may have been tied to chores. Or you may have been required to save all the money you received as gifts. Whatever your experiences, they may colour the way you look at allowances in general, so you need to try to put them aside. Even if you had to walk seven miles to school in blinding snow with a hole in your shoe, that doesn't mean you want the same thing for your own children.

Most people have no problem with the concept that teaching kids about money is an important part of their development. And most would acknowledge that having some money to manage is the best way to learn how money works. But when it comes to what you should ask of your children in exchange for that allowance, emotions can run pretty high.

Some people feel an allowance should have no strings attached. Others think it should be tied to chores in the home, school grades, or behaviour. ("If you don't smarten up, I'll cut off your allowance!") Some parents debate whether or not kids should work for their money by having part-time jobs. Some feel that school is a child's job and that any other work detracts from potential academic success. Others think that a part-time job is perfectly fine, while still others believe that a part-time job is essential because it begins the development of a good work ethic.

I believe that allowances should come strings-free and that it's perfectly fine for children to get a part-time job to supplement their allowance—not to replace it— when they get older.

Think about why you're giving your kid an allowance. The objective should be to teach him money-management skills. The fact that you work hard for your money will be brought home when your child learns relative value (which we'll discuss in the "Spending" chapter): how many hours he has to work to afford that pair of running shoes.

Money doesn't work as a reward for good behaviour. Just ask the many management theorists who have proven that money is not a motivator for adults. So why should it be for children? Good behaviour is based on an understanding of right and wrong, thoughtfulness, caring, and consideration, along with myriad other positive attributes, all of which have to be internalized.

Good grades are your child's responsibility. School is his primary job, and good grades are an indication that he is doing his job well. If you provide financial reward for good grades, you are externalizing the reward. Instead, the reward should be internalized: the self-esteem and pride that accompany having done well at school.

As for an allowance being payment for chores, who pays you to do the chores in your home? Chores are a part of each individual's responsibility to the family. Payment for regular chores negates a child's individual responsibility as a member of the family unit. (Payment for extra household tasks—those above and beyond a child's normal chores—is fine when your kid is specifically doing the task to earn some money.) The biggest problem in tying your child's allowance to the completion of chores comes on the day when you must withdraw the allowance because the chores haven't been completed. Now you're teaching your child, "I have the money, and you'll have to do as I say to get some of it!" That's a straight-out power play. "I have the money, so I have the power." Ouch! Not a lesson I want my children to learn. A far better tactic for teaching children who don't follow through on household responsibilities is to do a like-for-like comparison. "Kiddo, if you don't make your bed, I'm going to have to. And I only have time to do one thing, make your bed or make your lunch. Which one do you want to do?"

If you want to teach your children the value of working for pay, then that can easily be incorporated into your money lessons; it isn't a substitute for an allowance. As your children get older, they will be looking for ways to make more money. You can count on it. And this is where the work-for-pay learning comes in. Perhaps Kiddo is willing to take on the job of cleaning the kitty litter. Is it worth $5 a week to you to not have to do that job anymore? If it is, each week you fork over the $5, providing the kitty litter has been kept clean. A substandard job means you dock your worker's pay. No commitment to following through means Kiddo doesn't get paid. But if all goes well, you are saved from the nasty job, and Kiddo feels adequately rewarded. There are loads of things kids can do to earn money at home. From washing the car to weeding the garden, from shovelling the snow to cutting the grass, you'll always have jobs you can pay your kids to do for you if you want to teach the work-for-pay lesson.

As your child gets older, you'll review and adjust the amount he receives as an allowance. Pick a specific time of year—the beginning of the year, your child's birthday week, the beginning of a new school year—and make the review routine. If your son is looking for a hefty increase, ask him to give you a written proposal or a formal presentation explaining how much he wants and why. If you were asking for a raise at work, you'd have to justify your request. Perhaps he feels it is time he started buying his own clothes. You can negotiate the initial amount, outline the attached responsibilities, and implement the plan slowly. Moving from no clothing allowance to a year's clothing allowance in one fell swoop is a recipe for disaster. Let your child assume responsibility in small increments.

Before you do your allowance review, think about what you want to accomplish over the next year in teaching your child about money. Is it time to put your daughter on a clothing allowance? Should your son take on responsibility for managing the money spent on his soccer? Do you want your wee one to learn to accumulate a little each week to buy school supplies come the start of the new school year? Talk with your partner about how much responsibility you feel your child can take on. Perhaps you wish to start your daughter on an investment program. If so, you'll need to do a fair amount of teaching, and you'll need to up her allowance to take the money for investing into account. You'll also have to carefully monitor her progress to ensure the funds are being directed to the appropriate new category in her budget.

Keep Your Hand Out of Your Pocket

An allowance only works if, once given, you keep your hand out of your pocket. Giving an allowance backed up by the dole system is a great way to raise a Princess (male or female). If you want a responsible and in-dependent young adult, keep your hand out of your pocket and let the consequences of your child's behaviour teach some important lessons.

So what do you do if your daughter takes her monthly clothing allotment and blows it all on a dress for a party? So be it. The money is gone. If you can't stand seeing her in those ratty old jeans, that's your problem, not hers. At some point, you have to allow your children to be self-determining. If you object to your daughter showing up to special family gatherings wearing something you consider totally inappropriate, you can ask her to be considerate of your feelings and dress a little more conservatively. Take her shopping for a special outfit and set it aside for those occasions.

Can't stand to see your hard-earned money being spent on the trashy clothes she buys? It's not your money. It's her money. You gave it to her, and it's hers to manage. Let her live with the consequences of her purchase decisions. If she comes to you and says, "Mom, I don't have anything to wear! I need a decent dress," resist the urge to take her on a shopping spree out of sheer relief. If there are no consequences to her purchase decisions, she won't learn anything. She needs to experience the natural consequences. Your best response would be, "Molly, I'm sorry you don't think you have anything decent to wear. Maybe you should budget for some new clothes out of your next allowance."

Clothing is often a point of disagreement between parents and children. But there are hundreds of other examples. Your son may arrive home one day with a haphazard haircut that makes him look, at least from your perspective, like a barbarian. Grit your teeth and smile. Your daughter may decide to spend her long-saved planned spending money on something other than her original goal. That's her choice. Your son arrives home with a beat-up car on its last legs. And he paid what for it? You can say, "Get rid of that thing—you're not parking it in front of my house!" or you can say, "Have you considered what it will cost to find a parking place for that?"

The way you react to your children's purchase decisions will affect the way they continue to make their decisions. In a perfect world, your child would have your exquisite taste, ask for your advice on each purchase decision, and demonstrate a healthy helping of common sense in all things financial. But it's not a perfect world, and making mistakes is part of the process of learning about money.

When children make mistakes, you can rant and rave, which will win you no points as a balanced and open-minded parent; rush in and bail your kid out, which will do nothing in terms of teaching what may be a very important lesson in consequences; or help your child determine how to fix the problem.

If your daughter dents the car, she should not only have to pay for the repair, she should also have to take time from her busy schedule to have the repairs done. If your son spends $200 on a pair of running shoes (when a $50 pair would have been fine), he should have to go without whatever else that money was destined for: a school trip, a special purchase, or next month's supply of razors.

With your guidance, an allowance can be used to teach important lessons in borrowing and lending, the pleasure derived from generosity, how to be a good consumer, and the importance of considering those less fortunate.

2. Ages and Stages

One of the nice things about using an allowance guided, at least initially, by a child's age is that as your child gets older, he will get more money for which he has to be responsible. As you put more and more into his hands, you increase his level of responsibility and teach more complex ideas.

At age six, a young 'un only has to cope with a small amount of money and the simplest of wants. By age 12, more factors are driving your child's desire to consume, and a steadily growing allowance lets you help her increase her understanding of ideas like needs versus wants.

When Alex was 12, I started giving her a clothing allowance. We agreed that the money I gave her would cover all her clothing except outerwear (I didn't want her to skimp) and footwear (a pair of boots, a pair of running shoes, and two other pairs of shoes a year). She had to plan for everything else. When I told my friends I was giving my 12-year-old $50 a month for a clothing allowance, most of them freaked. That was an outrageous amount of money for a kid! What if she blew it on crap? Suppose she bought clothes I didn't approve of? Other than the stuff I said I would buy, and birthday and Christmas presents, I never had to put my hand in my wallet again: not for swimsuits or semi-formal dresses. (I did buy her prom dress.) Alex learned to accumulate money for more expensive things, shop on sale so she'd have money for accessories, and take care of her stuff.

When Alex was about 15, she got her first clothing allowance raise. She had never asked, but I thought it was time. She was growing like a weed. I asked how much she thought she needed. She said $100 a month. I laughed. We settled on $70. By the time she was 16, she was The Best Shopper. She indulged herself but knew her limits. And she definitely knew the difference between a want and a need. Kids grasp financial principles at different ages. Parents underestimate what their kids can understand, sometimes because they cannot even conceive of giving up any control.

But if you want your kids to be responsible, you must treat them with respect and give them some room to try, fail, and try again. Assess the level your child is at and teach lessons that can be learned, because Junior is ready to learn. And be willing to let your kids experience the learning for themselves. Show them how and then let them experiment. Learning from the natural consequences of our decisions is the best learning.

Here are some things to think about at various ages.

Toddlers

Try to be aware of what kids may be learning from you, even as toddlers. Pick up a penny on the sidewalk and you show that even the smallest denomination is valuable. Throw your change into a drawer, into a jar, into a box without explanation, and you teach your kids that small change is worthless to you, not worth your time and energy to sort and bank. As you pull cash from an ATM, take the time to explain that you had to work for that money, that you put it in the bank to keep it safe and earn interest, and that you can only take out as much as you have available. It doesn't matter that your child is a squirming three-year-old who is only interested in pushing the buttons. Talk to them about what you're doing with your money and why. Over time, your explanations will penetrate their youthful haze and they'll learn important lessons.

Four- to Six-Year-Olds

When your child is between the ages of four and six, introduce your young 'un to the basic concept that we use money to buy goods and services. Give your child the change to operate a vending machine or buy a newspaper. Explain that when you pay for something, the machine keeps the money, but you get the pop or newspaper (money is a means of exchange). You can progress from here to paying a cashier for small things like popsicles or candy. Ultimately, the message is that when you spend money, it's gone (money is an exhaustible resource). You get something in return. But you don't have the money anymore, so choose wisely.

Kids also need to learn that when you buy something, you'll be dipping into a finite amount of money. Give your child $3 to buy something the next time you go to the grocery store, and tell her she can choose just one thing. (Don't be surprised if your preschooler doesn't yet understand that there are 100 cents in a dollar. Helping her with the prices will be a great math lesson too.) This will show your child that money can be used up, so she has to choose carefully to get what she really wants.

Since busy people often run into stores to buy things, it's only natural for little ones to think, "When we go in a store, we buy something"—in your child's mind, anything at all. To counter this "store equals stuff" mentality, make a list before you go shopping, then show your child both your list and the money you have to pay for the items. Don't forget to do it when you hit the toy store for birthday party gifts too. This will help him see that some shopping trips are not about him.

Seven- to 10-Year-Olds

When your child is between the ages of seven and 10, you can start focusing your "money lessons" on deferral of gratification. Most parents are all too aware of the "see it, want it, gotta have it now" attitude. Lots of parents are happy to demonstrate it for their kids, so it's no wonder kids learn this lesson so well. Even if you are a planner, in all likelihood you haven't taken the time to explain this to your kids. So what they see is, "What Mommy wants, Mommy gets!"

Next time your child expresses an interest in buying a new doll or yet one more Lego kit, make a chart to help her see how long she has to save to get the money for the item. Find a picture that represents the item your child wishes to buy and paste it at the top of the chart. Draw boxes for the number of weeks she will have to save. So if the item costs $10 and she is setting aside $2 in her allowance for planned spending each week, you'll draw five boxes. Staple an envelope to the chart. Then, each week when you give her allowance to her, she'll put $2 into the envelope and mark off one of the boxes. This will show her that she can't always have what she wants right away. Sometimes it takes time to accumulate the money we need to buy the things we want.

It's important to teach kids to be discerning consumers. Ask your child to make a list of all the things he would buy if he had $100. Then ask him to choose the three items he considers most desirable and answer the following questions:

- What do I like about it?
- What don't I like about it?
- How long will I want to use it?
- What's the best price for it?

- How could I get it and spend less, or spend nothing at all?

Tell him that sometimes it's really easy to be attracted to an item because a friend has it or because it looks great on TV, but you need to think about why you want it, and if it'll do what you expect, before you buy it (more about this in the "Spending" chapter). Make trimming household expenses a family affair, and teach an important money lesson along the way. Assign your kids one or two responsibilities for meeting your household budget, things like turning off lights to save on electricity, or coming up with a list of grocery items for their lunches so they waste less food. Any money you save can go towards a family goal, such as a new computer or a vacation. This will show your kids that balancing today's needs with tomorrow's wants sometimes means you have to find ways to spend less money.

Eleven- to 14-Year-Olds

It's time to explode the myth of the bottomless wallet. To some children, parents with regular salaries seem rich. It doesn't matter if we say we have no money. They don't believe us. We have those credit cards. And then there are those cheques. To demonstrate just how little disposable income is left after expenses are met, ask your child to:

- List 10 things he thinks you have to pay for.
- Estimate how much each costs.
- Estimate how much you earn.

Now, go over the figures and fill in the gaps or correct the misperceptions. I remember the first time I pointed to a load of firewood (we had a wood-burning furnace at the time) and asked Alex what she thought I'd paid for the wood. She assessed the pile and then said, "$137." (I smile even now at the not-round number she came up with.) I laughed and said, "Higher." She guessed again. "Higher." Her eyes widened and she finally said, "I don't want to do this anymore."

"That pile of wood," I said, pointing to a mountain that still had to be stacked, "will heat our house for half the winter and cost $750." She was aghast. How could she possibly know if we didn't have the conversation? The same holds true for what you pay for hydro, to cover your property taxes, for your mortgage, to insure your car.

Wherever possible, show your child a bill to make the cost concrete. Total up the expenses. (You'll also have to introduce the costs you pay less regularly, like insurance, dental bills, and holidays.) Deduct it from your net income. Decide together what to do with what's really left for entertainment—take in a movie or hit McDonald's for lunch. (For very concrete or hands-on learners, consider using stacks of Monopoly money to show your children how the cash flows out, and just how quickly.)

Many parents are hugely resistant to telling their children how much they make and where the money goes. Some say that money is a private matter. So private that you can't talk to your own children about it? Or is your unwillingness to do this because your own financial foundation is crumbling? What better motivation is there to fix your mess than to be able to launch your kids with a firm foundation of their own?

Some parents say they don't want to rob their kids of their innocence. Don't think you're preserving their innocence by not teaching them about money. What you're preserving is their ignorance. And, perhaps, your power. Innocence isn't the issue. Since there's nothing inherently bad, dirty, or evil about money, innocence shouldn't come into the equation. How are kids to understand why you can't order pizza every night if they don't understand how that would blow the budget?

To give your child some experience living within the parameters of your family budget, assign her dinner responsibilities one night of the week, along with one-seventh of the dinner budget. Perhaps your food budget allows for $20 per family dinner. Perhaps less. Whatever the amount, she'll have to come up with a plan, look at what's already in the cupboard and the fridge, and then come with you to the market to choose the items for dinner that night. She must plan a balanced and delicious meal. Dessert would be nice too.

Choose an activity your child likes to do, such as piano, baseball, or renting movies. Put the amount of money, divided by 52, into your child's regular allowance and explain that he must set that amount aside each week for his music lessons, Little League fees, or video rentals. Tell him there are lots of things we have to plan for before we can pay for them, and that means setting aside a little money each week to cover the costs. You can use labelled jars or envelopes to store the planned spending money.

This is also the stage at which most kids can deal with the more abstract idea of a debit card. Now that they are consuming more on their own (without you), a debit card means they won't have to walk around with a wad of cash in their wallets. If you've started your children on a clothing allowance or they are now responsible for their own back-to-school shopping, using a debit card may not only be more convenient but may offer the opportunity to teach important lessons about tracking their spending.

Fifteen and Older

By the time your child is in grade 10, he is likely old enough for lessons on long-term savings and investing. Savings options like RRSPs and TFSAs can help teach kids the difference between short-term (I'm spending this money imminently) accumulation, which I like to call "planned spending," and long-term (I'm not going to touch this money no matter what) savings.

Another lucrative lesson children can learn from tax-deferred savings plans is the one about compounding return. Find a savings calculator on the Internet and take your child through the exercise of saving a specific amount of money over the long term. You might, for example, use saving just $100 a month at 5% for 20, 30, and 40 years to show that more time means hugely different amounts accumulated. Then change the rate of return from 5% to 7% to show how increasing your rate of return grows your money even faster. Unlike saving, taxes aren't intuitive, so you have to explain why they're necessary, how they're calculated, and how much less you have to live on after they are paid. There are sites online that will calculate both average and marginal tax rates; find one and show your almost-adult how $35,000, $50,000, and $75,000 in income means less money in the bank than you might think once income taxes have been deducted.

Whether your kids are shovelling snow, walking dogs, or babysitting, as long as they get a social insurance number, keep their financial information straight, and file a tax return to qualify their earned income, they can begin to contribute to an RRSP. Since they don't have much in the way of taxable income, they can hold their deductions for later years when they are paying more tax and could use a break. Still pay your bills by cheque? Let your kids write them out. Pay bills online? Show them how it's done and let them pay some bills. Developing a comfort level with the things adults do as a matter of course means they won't panic when they have to do it for themselves. The first couple of times Alex had to enter her PIN for a debit purchase, she was in a twist. What if she entered it wrong? What if it didn't work? What if the purchase was denied because she was over her limit? All those anxieties opened doors to very good conversations, and the practice means she doesn't have to think twice now that she's on her own at school.

If you're considering one of those prepaid credit cards that are becoming popular, don't. Prepaid credit cards are preloaded with money your kid can spend, and they are permission to go shopping. They are more like gift cards than like credit cards—they never need repayment, and dontcha just want to teach kids that! Teaching kids about credit is an important part of rounding out their financial educations, so that's what we'll talk about next.

3. Credit

Some people think that credit cards are evil and that keeping kids on the other side of the moat is the only way to keep them safe. But that assumes that credit card companies will never breach the castle. Hey, it's only a matter of time. Far better that kids know what to do with plastic when they finally have some in their hot little hands. And who better to teach them than you?

The first time most kids learn about credit is when they go off to university and the credit card companies start throwing cards at them. With no experience and very little understanding of the long-term negative ramifications, kids start to charge. And they charge, charge, charge until they're in a hole. That's because they've had no prior experience with how a credit card works or how to use one so that it's a tool and not a Debt Pit.

All it takes is a little time and a thoughtful approach to help your children see credit for what it is: useful when used correctly, deadly when it isn't. When you use your credit card to purchase gas or pay for a new bathing suit, take the time to explain how credit cards work. Show your children that you're only putting on the card what you can afford to pay off when the bill arrives. Explain that you use your card for good reasons, not just to scratch your consumer itch, because this debt has to be repaid.

Even relatively young kids can get in on this lesson. Issue your 10-year-old a credit card on the Bank of Mom & Dad. (Have her design it herself, if you like.) Draw up a cardholder's agreement that both of you sign. It should clearly state:

- How much credit she can use: "Charges can be made to this card up to a credit limit of $40."
- When the statement will arrive: "Statements will arrive on the 15th of each month."
- The date by which it must be paid—called the "grace period": "Payments must be made by the 30th of each month."
- The minimum payment required: "The minimum payment is 25% of the outstanding balance."

- How much interest will be charged if the balance is not paid off in full: "If the balance is not paid in full and on time, interest will be charged on the entire balance at a rate of 25% a year, or 2% a month."

It's important that you use a fairly high interest rate in your agreement. If you wuss out and charge just 5% a year, the lesson that using someone else's money can be expensive is likely to get lost. Charge a whopping amount of interest (hey, department stores charge more than 24%), and the lesson will be made more real for your kids.

Your child can now use her credit card when she goes shopping with you. If she sees something she wants to buy, she gives you her card and you make the purchase on her behalf using your money. You give her a charge receipt. Remind her that if she doesn't have the money at home ready to pay the card off in full when the bill comes in, she'll have to allocate her future allowance (or babysitting money) to pay the bill when it arrives. Make the point clear: she is spending money she hasn't yet earned, and she'll pay interest to do so if she can't come up with the money in time.

If she spends more than she can afford or makes her payments late, you'll have to charge her interest on the balance. Use 24% as your interest rate for this exercise and don't give in. To calculate the interest, multiply her monthly balance by 2% (which is the equivalent of 24% a year). So if she owes $16.50, the calculation would look like this: $16.50 \times 2 \div 100 = \$0.33$.

Point out that she is paying that 33¢ for having used your money for a month. It is like she "rented" the $16.50 for a month, and the cost was 33¢. And if she doesn't pay it off soon, it will continue to cost her money every month to keep "renting" the money she's charged on her credit card.

Once your child is 16 or so (you'll have to gauge his maturity), you may wish to get him an actual credit card (it will have to be in your name since only those 18 and older can have a credit card of their own) and start him using it and repaying it regularly. This is a habit, and one well worth the effort to form. By the time your child is 18, he should have a card in his own name so he can start building a credit history.

As you teach your credit lessons, don't skip steps because you think they should be obvious to your teen-ager. Start by explaining how credit cards work.

1. Emphasize the connection between charging one month and paying the next: "Since there is a lag between when you use the card and when you must actually pay for the purchases you made, it is easy to forget what you bought. You need to keep track of what you're buying and what you owe so that you know you'll have the money to pay the balance when the bill comes in. Here's a notebook to help you keep track."

2. Stress that credit is not "free money" unless the balance is paid in full before the grace period expires: "If you leave so much as $1 as a balance on the card, you will have to pay interest ON THE ENTIRE BALANCE. Remember, you're just 'renting' someone else's money, and they want their rental fee."

3. Explain interest and how it compounds if a debt piles up. For this you can go to the Internet. Find a credit card repayment calculator and put in a balance of $1,000. Choose an interest rate of 24% and the minimum monthly payment option. Then let the calculator do its work to show how much interest will build up on the card over time.

4. Read the fine print and review key terms such as late fees and over-balance charges: "If you're late with a payment, the credit card company sees that as an opportunity to make more money, so they make you pay an extra fee. And if you go over your balance, that's another opportunity for them to make you pay."

5. Talk about how to keep the card safe and what to do if it's stolen or lost: "If you lend anyone your credit card or share your code, you're asking to be a victim of identity theft, which is where someone else pretends to be you, shops up a storm, and leaves you responsible for paying it all off. No one else should have access to your card. Keep it somewhere safe, don't leave your wallet lying around or in a car, and protect your credit identity. If you think you've lost your card or that it's been stolen, report it immediately. You won't be charged for purchases made if you've reported it. If you haven't, you're on the hook for whatever has been put on the card."

6. Set limits and monitor your child's use of the card. He must prove his ability to handle the low limit you've established—$100 is good to start—before you increase his responsibility. When he is old enough and ready for a card in his own name, encourage him to shop around for low rates and fees.

7. Discuss the importance of a good credit history and how a bad one can get in the way of future borrowing, whether your child needs to buy a car, rent an apartment, or get a mortgage for a house: "A good credit history is like a passport. It lets you get access to other people's money for things you wish to finance. But a bad credit history is like a wall: you'll pay a lot of money to get over it, assuming there's a ladder tall enough. If you ruin your credit history by not being responsible and not paying on time, you'll limit your options later."

8. Show your child how to get a copy of her credit report, which can be accessed for free once a year at each of Canada's two credit bureaus, TransUnion

and Equifax. Go online and look them up to show your child what can be found on a credit bureau report. The lessons your children learn about plastic at home will stick with them through life. (Well, we can cross our fingers, right?) It's a better option than the alternative. There are so many people who really don't know how to use credit appropriately, all because they never developed the discipline of self-regulation through practice.

Not all kids will be suited to using plastic. Not all adults should be using plastic. Be honest about your kids' organization and sense of discipline. If Molly just doesn't have the wherewithal to manage credit smartly, tell her that she isn't well suited to using credit cards and that, until she develops some discipline, she should avoid them like the plague.

Your own values will also come into play when it comes to teaching kids about how to spend money. Whether your family lives on cash or uses plastic, talk with your children about the choices you've made and why. And remember that they're always watching, so be mindful of how your use of plastic influences your children.

Advances and Loans

Whenever I talk about allowances, inevitably questions come up about whether or not I think giving kids loans or advances on their allowances is a good idea. In this case, we're not talking about a lesson in credit so much as a way of managing kids' expectations and behaviours. My take on it is that it's really a matter of personal choice. However, there are some things you should think about when making the decision. Each occasion will warrant consideration on its own merit—there are no hard-and-fast rules—and every experience has the potential to teach a lesson, good or bad.

How often does your kid hit you up for money? If Boyo is always asking for an advance or loan, he may be having trouble learning how to budget and how to plan for the future. Adults manifest the same lack of skill when, rather than saving for an item, they apply for a loan or use their credit card and carry a balance. The desire for immediate gratification outweighs their patience in implementing a planned spending approach. However, the cost of this borrow-spend-repay strategy is very high. Every cent in interest paid on a loan (including on a credit card balance) is money wasted. So, do you want your child to become a borrower or to be skilled at planned spending? If Boyo doesn't ask for a loan or advance with any regularity—if it really is a case of an emergency or a special occasion—then using it as a lesson on how to borrow, and the costs associated, can be worthwhile.

What are your expectations in giving the loan?
If you go to a bank to borrow money, you're expected to pay the money back. All of it. Not only will the lenders expect you to repay the principal, they'll also expect you to ante up some interest. And you have to make your payments on time. If you want your child to learn about borrowing, you need to set some expectations.

Are you going to charge interest?
Now don't come hissing and clawing at me with terms like "usury" and "profit." I'm not suggesting you build your retirement plan on the back of your child's borrowing. I am suggesting that if you want children to experience the true impact of using someone else's money to meet their spending desires, then interest must be a part of the equation. With the lack of cost would go the deterrent to borrow (as small a deterrent as it sometimes appears to be). If you teach them it costs nothing

more to acquire that scooter than the ticket price, even when they're tying up your hard-earned money, are you really preparing them for the credit cards and personal lines of credit that are in their futures? If this is to be a real money lesson, charge them 24%, which translates easily into 2% a month.

What if Sweet Pea won't repay the loan or allowance advance?

Make the point that inconsistent repayment affects a person's ability to borrow in the future. If she doesn't repay the loan, there will be no future borrowing. You may decide to withhold a part of her allowance and apply that to the repayment of the loan. (In the real world, this is referred to as having your wages "garnished.") But before you take this step, think of the message you are sending by removing the responsibility for making the repayment from your child. A better lesson would be to insist upon repayment as soon as you have given your child her allowance. Create a chart showing how much she owes. Then each week reduce the amount owed so she can see her progress in repaying the loan.

Let's say your daughter wanted to buy a new gaming system. She had saved $65 of the $185 she needed.

There was a great sale on, and she got the item for $145, with a loan of $80 from you. Now that she has the game, you're having trouble getting her to pay you back. Time to make the chart.

At 24% a year in interest (which works out to 2% a month), your kid's $80 loan will cost ($80 × 2 ÷ 100) $1.60 a month, or 40¢ a week, in interest. If you expect that loan to be paid off in five weeks, then she'd also have to give you back ($80 ÷ 5) $16 a week towards the principal (the amount you lent her). So you would draw up a chart that looks like this:

	Interest	Principal	Total Payment	Still Owed
Week 1	40¢	$16	$16.40	$64
Week 2	40¢	$16	$16.40	$48
Week 3	40¢	$16	$16.40	$32
Week 4	40¢	$16	$16.40	$16
Week 5	40¢	$16	$16.40	$0

If your child is wishy-washy in keeping her commitments—she repays the loan eventually, but at her own pace and with a fair amount of grumbling—there's fallout: before you will give her another loan, she must offer you some form of collateral. It may be her bike, her telephone, or her laptop. Make up a loan agreement and include a paragraph that clearly spells out that if the loan is not repaid on time, you have the right to take whatever collateral she has given you until the loan is repaid.

A child who does not repay a loan on time needs to see the consequence of developing a bad credit history: no more loans. And the child who is constantly borrowing may benefit from having a loan request declined, to teach how constant borrowing reduces her ability to repay (and therefore qualify for) yet another loan.

Borrowing itself isn't a bad thing, provided that we're borrowing for the right reasons. Knowing when to borrow and how to manage credit are important lessons well worth a few discussions at home where they can be learned in safety.

4. Saving

As a culture, we have lost the knack of saving. We know we should. And we keep meaning to. But we are completely out of the habit. If you want your children to grow up knowing the value of saving, starting the habit early is key. Like brushing their teeth and saying "please" and "thank you," saving can become something they do automatically because the habit was introduced early.

Some kids are natural-born savers. My son, Malcolm, is a prime example. He doesn't have a lot of "wants," so he finds it easy to squirrel away his allowance week after week. And since he enjoys watching his stash of cash grow, spending money requires a big motivation. For many kids, however, saving is something that has to be learned. Regardless of your current predisposition to saving, you are your children's most influential teacher.

So you may want to look at the example you are setting.

Saving is as easy as ABC: make saving Automatic, Bury the savings, and be Consistent. Teaching your children the ABCs of saving may make the difference between a child who has a good savings ethic and one who spends every red cent he makes because he's never learned to defer gratification.

A: Automatic Savings

When people decide to save what's left over after expenses, very little goes into the savings account. Smart savers pay themselves first each month. And they set a definite amount and date to save. For kids, the savings habit starts when you introduce them to the idea of putting 10% of everything they get in the way of allowance or earnings into a Savings Jar or bank account. Started early in life, this habit becomes a natural part of managing money. And it's a habit that will serve your children well for the rest of their lives.

B: Bury the Money

"Out of sight, out of mind" is the mantra for successful saving for those for whom the temptation to spend is powerful. Kids will soon find a good reason to spend the money left in their wallets, just as their parents find it easy to spend the money left in their chequing accounts. For young children, the ritualized act of putting that money in a container from which it is not taken on a whim creates a strong sense that money saved is untouchable—exactly what's needed for a savings program to be successful. For older kids who are working, moving money from their regular account to a savings account achieves the same end. Encourage your child to set up a separate savings account and to transfer a specific percentage of the money they are earning into that account each time they are paid.

The year before Alex headed off to university, she got her first real job as a cashier in a grocery store. We had The Talk about how much she would need for university and what I expected her to kick in. I asked her how much she thought she'd need to save to hit the mark. She decided that each time she was paid, she would transfer 85% of whatever she received to her savings account. That way it wouldn't be where she could get at it with her debit card. Out of sight, out of mind!

I have had friends question my insistence that Alex pay part of her university costs. They think because I'm in a position to cover the whole thing, I should. I don't see it quite the same way. If Alex wants a university education, she should be willing to put some sweat into getting one. I think kids are far less likely to blow their year on booze and partying if they had to stand for hours behind a cash register dealing with people and bagging groceries. I was upfront with my girl. If she didn't have the get-up-and-go to earn her fair share, I wasn't prepared to pony up my share. As long as she was taking her education seriously, I would be happy to help. I think that sometimes, as parents, we take our role in the relationship so much to heart that we undermine our children's need to be part of the process and contribute. How can they value what they've never had to work hard to have?

If you want your children to save for their education, you can't assume that it's just going to happen. You have to talk about it. You have to set some expectations, offer suggestions for a plan of action, and follow up to see if they're following through.

If your child refuses to save anything for their post-secondary schooling—hey, isn't that what student loans are for?—take them through the numbers. Show them what it will cost for each year they are in school, including tuition, living expenses, books, transportation, and the like. Show them how much debt they will graduate with if they have to borrow everything they need. Show them what the interest rate will be on their student loans (you can get this off the Internet), how much interest they'll pay in total, and how much of their monthly earnings they'll have to commit to paying off that debt.

C: Consistency

Remember the story about the tortoise and the hare? It's the regular, steady, ongoing additions that add up. Quick starts and stops are difficult to manage and bring far less of a sense of personal satisfaction. But a slow and steady approach to saving will win every time. That's why it's so important to encourage your children to embrace the Save 10% Rule. If they get $6 a week as an allowance, they save 60¢ a week. If they're working and earning $75 a week, they save $7.50. Eventually it becomes a "no-brainer." They save because they have internalized the rule. And over time, those slow and steady savings add up.

When Kids Won't Save

If your child just can't seem to save, you'll need to do some digging to determine where the problem lies.

Maybe she has expenses that keep cropping up that are throwing her best efforts off. Help your child re-evaluate her spending plan. Perhaps she is simply not receiving enough allowance to meet all her needs.

Or perhaps she's not spending consciously or tracking her money, so she's spending money that's already allocated to a bill. If, for example, she's responsible for her own cell phone bill but went shopping and spent the money on a new pair of shoes, that's an example of poor planning. Hey, your kid's human, and she may be giving in to many of the same consumer pressures you feel. You need to identify the problem and talk about a solution such as using a spending journal to track where her money is going. What you should NOT do is freak out or rant about how irresponsible she is. She's learning. And there will be bumps along the way. To deal with the unpaid bill, point out that paying the bill must now be Priority One before money is spent on anything else. Then, using the spending journal, show her how to debit expenses she knows she must deal with before she can decide how much money she has to go shopping.

Motivating Kids to Save

Saving can be surprisingly easy and rewarding for children. It helps them to develop a sense of security and mastery over their money. They can see the results of their discipline and efforts as their account balances grow. And as they accumulate savings, they begin to see their money earning greater and greater amounts on its own. "With our pathetic rates of interest?" you ask disbelievingly. Well, you may have to step in here to make the point a little more exciting for your kids.

One of the most effective ways of motivating a child to get into the savings habit is with a savings-matching program. You offer to match every dollar your child saves within a specific period of time with a dollar of your own. Alternatively, you might offer to match her savings if she can save a specific amount by a certain date. "Molly, now that you're working regularly (or getting a higher allowance), you may want to consider saving a little more of your money. Here's the deal. If you can save $60 by the end of the summer, I'll match that amount so you can begin investing."

A savings-matching program is an excellent way to inspire children to stay focused on long-term goals. How you choose to implement the program will be a matter of personal preference. You might decide that if your daughter saves her first year's university tuition, you'll spring for her second and third years. Or if your son decides to travel the world, you'll spring for his Eurail pass or some other part of the trip. What's important is that your child set a goal and actively work towards achieving that goal, and that you support these efforts.

Kids Who Want to Save It All

If you have a child who never spends his allowance, who wants to save it all, you have a problem. If you don't have one of these children, you probably can't imagine this being a problem. And if you've been bragging about the fact that your son saves every penny, you'll resist thinking of this as a problem. But it is a problem nonetheless.

I have one of these. My son, Malcolm, doesn't have a lot of "wants." Given his druthers, he'd pile his money up in his wallet, never spending a cent. He puts away his formal "savings," just as Alex does, but he also hangs onto the money he should be spending. I actually stopped his allowance for over a year. The conversation went like this:

"Do you know why I give you an allowance?"

"Yeah."

"It's so that you can learn to manage money. If you never spend any of the money I give you, you're not managing it. You're just piling it up."

"So?"

"So, until you start using your money, you really have no need for money. So I'm stopping your allowance. When you tell me you need money, we'll start it up again."

When the time came, Malcolm came to me and said, "Mom, I need some money."

"What for?" I asked hopefully.

"To buy stuff."

"What kind of stuff?"

"You know, stuff. Like a new game for my DS."

"Okay," I said. "I'll restart your allowance. Do you remember the rules?"

"We may have to go over them again," he said, so we did. And he's been saving, sharing, and spending ever since. He still doesn't blow through money at the same clip as his sister, but at least he's learning that the point of money is to get the things we need and want, even as we stash some of our cash for tomorrow.

If you have a child who is hesitant to spend, you have to encourage her to use her money and show her how to derive pleasure from spending. Suggest that it's her turn to buy the ice-cream cones. Offer to buy the movie tickets if she'll buy the popcorn. Encourage her to think about things she wants, things that would give her pleasure. Don't worry about breaking her out of the savings habit. You'll keep reinforcing that by using the Save 10% Rule. But make sure she learns that the purpose of money is to pay for the things we need and to enjoy at least some of the things we want. Money is for saving AND for spending. We'll talk about how best to manage the spending side of the equation next.

5. Spending

Spending is a significant part of money management, so it makes sense to try to help kids figure out the best ways to use their money. Since children don't have "needs" on which they must spend money on a regular basis, it means taking the time to explain how needs and wants are different. For kids, everything is pretty much a want. And yet they come to think of those wants as needs, which is how they end up not being able to make the distinction later.

The fact that nobody clarified "needs" and "wants" for us, or taught most of us about smart shopping, is evident in the way we abuse plastic. More than half of North America's credit card holders have balances owing, paying what can be exorbitant interest rates for products and services that typically fall into the "wants" category and that may not even outlive their repayment schedules. Think dinners out, movie tickets, a party dress, or the latest technology toy.

While our values are very different from those of our parents, who typically spent only what they had, our "consumeritis" exists in large part because the money game has changed. It is in our generation that credit has become a substitute for disposable income. This has allowed some people to fall into the trap of thinking they can have it all at the same time. The result? Our generation has managed to rack up record levels of debt, and we are spending bazillions of dollars in interest every year because we've become such rabid consumers. If you don't want your children to fall into the consumeritis trap, you need to help them distinguish between the things that are Must-Haves and the things that are Nice-to-Haves.

Whether we are aware of it or not, we already play an important role in teaching our kids how to shop. Each time we hit the mall, we model what a consumer looks like. And whether our model is positive or not, our kids are learning. Teaching our children about becoming smart consumers may mean looking closely at our own spending patterns and developing some new habits. Teaching our children also requires that we take an active role in explaining what we are doing and why. And that's where relative value comes into play.

Relative Value

Relative value refers to the relationship between what an item costs and what you have to do to pay for it. If it costs $140 for a concert ticket, and after all your Must-Have expenses are met you're left with a disposable income of $5 an hour, you would have to work for 28 hours—or more than half a work week—to be able to afford that concert ticket. That puts a whole new spin on the real cost of that ticket.

As your children's primary financial guide, you have to look for ways to bring home the lesson of relative value. If your child has a job, talk about relative value in terms of how many papers have to be delivered, how many lawns have to be cut, or how many babysitting jobs have to be done relative to the cost of an item.

Let's say that your young lad has a job cutting grass for the neighbours in the summer. He cuts about five lawns a week, earning $25 per cut. He's pulling in $125 a week. Now let's say that he decides he has to have a new laptop. It's the fruity kind that costs about $1,700.

How many lawns does Laddie have to cut to pay for the laptop? Here's the math: $1,700 \div \$25/\text{lawn} = 68$. Yup, he'd have to cut 68 lawns to buy the laptop (not including tax). Put another way, he'd have to work for almost 14 weeks (methinks that's the whole summer!) to pay for that laptop ($1,700 \div \$125/\text{week} = 13.6$ weeks).

Now, here comes the hard part. It's time to share your own financial reality with your mini-me. Don't go screaming from the room. What are you afraid of? If you aren't prepared to share your personal financial circumstances with your kid, why should he listen to your money advice? Tell Junior how much money you make per hour; if you aren't paid by the hour, work it out. Deduct your total expenses from your net monthly income, and then divide by the number of hours you work each month to show your remaining disposable income per hour. So if you put $2,600 a month into the bank and you spend $2,250 to cover your living expenses, you have $350 a month left. Assuming you work a 40-hour week for four weeks a month, your disposable income is ($350 \div [40 \times 4]$) $2.19 an hour.

Now it's time to go shopping. Tell your child to pretend she has your hourly disposable income to spend on that new computer. Ask her to choose a computer she would like to have and write down the price. (You can make this as simple as a look through the ads in the newspaper or as detailed as a visit to one or two stores.) Divide the price by the hourly disposable income amount to show how many hours she would have to work to buy the computer. Ask your child if she would be prepared to work that many hours for that specific computer. If she chose a less expensive one, how many hours would she have to work?

Repeat the exercise with a holiday purchase, the purchase of a new TV, a snowmobile, a bicycle, or whatever is the "hot buy" in your kid's mind. But resist the urge to make every purchase into a lesson. Teaching relative value shouldn't be arduous. Opportunities will naturally arise when you can reinforce the concept. Don't lecture. Teach.

Fending Off Influences to Shop

Studies show that, on average, we're exposed to 3,000 ads per day, everywhere from the obvious media sources like TV and radio to the less obvious gas pumps and washroom stalls. Advertising is impossible to avoid. Houses are now being wrapped in ads, and companies are even looking at placing ads in space that will be visible from

Earth. I kid you not. It's your job as an aware parent to offset the barrage of messages your kids receive so that life doesn't become about being driven to buy the new hot Stuff.

Challenge your children's definition of "cool" by asking them how they feel about not owning something all the other kids have. Discuss how Stuff impacts on their sense of self. Would people like them more if they owned a certain item? Would people like them more if their face, body, skin, or hair looked different? Does an ad (and show them an ad targeting teens) make them feel that they'd be more popular if they bought whatever the ad was selling? If they say "yes" to any of these questions, talk about how important it is to have a sense of your own self that is not dictated by others. You can spend a lot of time and money to create an image you think is more attractive to others. Ultimately, however, you can't please everyone, and if you let yourself be dictated to by the cultural icons that set trends, you're just a wannabe. This isn't a "money" issue. This is an issue of self-esteem, and your job as a parent is to help your children develop a clear sense of who they are so they aren't unduly influenced by marketing tactics.

Encourage smart shopping by challenging advertisers' claims about their products. Do your own blind taste tests at home. Point out how the packaging influences the desire to buy and discuss whether what's contained in the package is all that different from the less expensive alternative. Celebrate Buy Nothing Day at home and use it to talk about why we often buy things we don't need, and how we can become smarter consumers and better savers.

Put shopping into perspective by explaining that shopping isn't a hobby or pastime. It's something we should be doing consciously. So we shop with a list, and we don't buy anything that's not on the list. And we shop with a budget, but we always look for ways to save, so we can put what we successfully keep in our pockets to work for us in our savings.

Most importantly, understand your own motivations to consume and walk the talk. Demonstrate how much more important it is to experience things together than it is to accumulate more stuff. Don't make up for the time you can't spend with your kids because of work or school or whatever else is making demands on your life by buying them whatever crap they say they want. If you use Stuff as a substitute, you'll be teaching your kids the wrong lessons. Focus on keeping money in the right place in your life, and help your children understand the role money should play in theirs.

Conclusion

Think back to the effort, patience, and time it took to potty train your beautiful toddler. Remember the effort, patience, and time it took to teach your child how to ride a bicycle, skate, or swim. Money management is the term for a whole bunch of individual skills wrapped up in one neat package. But each of the skills needs to be introduced, practised, and reinforced. And each takes time to acquire.

By the time your children go to university or college, they will have already learned a lot from you about money. Even if you choose not to take an active role in teaching your children about money, they will learn most of what they take into their future lives from what you do (as opposed to what you say). If you save regularly, they will see saving as an important part of money management. If you are an avid investor, they will develop an interest in investing. If you regularly donate to charity, your children will learn to share. An honest, straightforward approach to explaining money matters works best. Don't take the easy way out. "I don't have the money to buy you that thingamajig" as a pat answer to each request teaches little. Instead, use each opportunity to teach the important lessons of budgeting, relative value, prioritizing, and patience.

Your kids will know whether you are an impulse shopper or a planned spender, whether you are generous or miserly with your money, whether you see money as a tool or as a god. If you comparison-shop, they will learn from you. If you place a strong value on expensive brands, they will hear your message, even if those messages are mixed.

From early on, children receive multiple messages about money. At home they hear one thing; at school and among their peers they hear another. Mom does it one way; Dad is the complete opposite. What is consistent is that nobody seems able to agree on the money rules. And often those mixed messages stay with kids long after your parental influence has passed.

I knew a couple who were distinct opposites when it came to money. The father was a generous spirit who bought on impulse and loved to satisfy his children's every wish. The mother was a tightwad, begrudging most spending. The father's attitude was, "Money is a tool for making our lives more comfortable." The mother's attitude was, "We don't have enough money." The father gave his children money to buy gifts for loved ones. The mother expected her children to fund their gift-giving themselves. The messages this couple's children received were very mixed. While that's pretty usual for many families, it doesn't help to promote learning, since inconsistent messages are confusing for children. If you are teaching your children about money as a couple, it's important you develop a joint plan about what you will teach.

Differences in style are natural. How you demonstrate those differences to your kids will have an impact on the lessons they eventually put to use in their own lives. Talk about how you want to teach your children the important money lessons. Starting from a shared belief—even if only in the basic ground rules—will go a long way to delivering a consistent message to your children. If you've decided not to leave your children's financial education to whoever comes along with a good story to tell, if you've decided you want to pass along your values, if you're determined that your children should not make the same mistakes you did, then you're ready to step into the role of raising Money-Smart Kids.

Your Role in Raising Money-Smart Kids

Here are 10 simple rules that apply not only to teaching kids about money but also to teaching kids about life.

Rule #1: Remember that your children are always watching you.

You know that old saying, "Do as I say, not as I do"? Well, kids learn from what you do. Shop without a list, and they'll learn that when you go into a store, it's okay to impulse shop.

Rule #2: It's just as easy to learn bad habits as good ones.

Browsing serves a purpose. Unfortunately, in our time-pressured world, we haul our kids in and out of stores, seemingly without purpose, always buying something. If you never leave a store without buying SOMETHING, your kids will quickly learn that their purpose in going into a store is to find something to buy. You can't then turn around and say, "Do you think we always have to buy something?" Because the answer is, "Yes." That's what you've taught them. A bad habit. And all because you didn't follow . . .

Rule #3: Explain everything you're doing.

Yes, it can become tedious, so it doesn't have to be EVERYTHING, just most things. You can't take cash from a cash machine without explaining how it works or your kids will think, "The machine just gives you money." You can't write a cheque without explaining how it works or your kids will think, "Cheques are money." You can't leave a tip on a table without explaining what you're doing or your kids will think, "Mommy forgot money on the table. I better pick it up."

Rule #4: What goes around comes around.

If you're truthful with your children, you have the right to expect the same from them. But if you lie, obfuscate, and only tell part of the story, why would you expect any better from them? Think you can pull one over on your kids? Go back and read Rules #1 and #2 again.

Rule #5: Keep it simple.
The more complicated you make something, the harder it is to learn. Complicated rules for how kids can get and use their money are hard to understand and keep straight. The reason the Magic Jars work so well (for both kids and adults) is that the system is simple to understand and easy to use.

Rule #6: Don't try to do too much at once.
Kids need down time to just hang, think, imagine, process, cope. Jamming a whole bunch of money lessons into a day, week, or month won't work, since time is important for practising and processing.

Rule #7: Prepare your kids.
Telling your kids what you're going to do helps them create a mind-map of what's going to happen. Ditto teaching them about money. Lay out what you'll be teaching them before you get into the actual lesson so they know what to expect. If you're going to talk about allowances, tell them you're not going to get into loans, advances, work-for-pay, or all the other stuff that can make the discussion really complicated—you're just going to be talking about how much, how often, and what they can do with their money.

Rule #8: Be prepared.

Just as you wouldn't dream of heading out without a bag of cleanup stuff and a set of nibblies to hold your child's hunger at bay, you also have to be prepared when you're teaching kids about money. Don't try giving a kid her $7 allowance using a five and two loonies. How will she put away her 70¢ for saving or divvy up money between her planned spending (for that new CD) and her mad money?

Rule #9: Routine is your friend.

Keep switching the day when you give the allowance and watch your kid eye you suspiciously. Forget to give the allowance and you'll prove you're not trustworthy. Change the rules on how the allowance can be used based on every new situation and you'll teach your kids that they can change the rules too—as long as they can come up with a good justification!

Rule #10: Know when to let go.

It's not worth all the hassle to get on your kids' cases about everything. Know when to let things go and just relax. As long as you deliver a consistent message, love them, and have their best interests at heart, they'll turn out fine. If you're doing anything "because of the principle of the thing," it's because you're too lazy to weigh each decision on its own merit.

Children progress pretty quickly from bubble gum to fancy jeans. While the dollar amounts they spend rise dramatically as they age, their respect for money doesn't automatically increase proportionately. Only by helping them to learn the important money lessons will they develop the appropriate attitudes towards money. Good luck, and remember that lessons learned with laughter last longer!

Don't miss these other essential books
by Gail Vaz-Oxlade